EcoWorks

HOW RECYCLING WORKS

Geoff Barker

Gareth Stevens
Publishing

Please visit our website, www.garethstevens.com. For a free color catalog of all our high-quality books, call toll free 1-800-542-2595 or fax 1-877-542-2596.

Library of Congress Cataloging-in-Publication Data

Barker, Geoffrey.
How recycling works / by Geoffrey Barker.
  p. cm. — (EcoWorks)
Includes index.
ISBN 978-1-4339-9565-1 (pbk.)
ISBN 978-1-4339-9566-8 (6-pack)
ISBN 978-1-4339-9564-4 (library binding)
1. Salvage (Waste, etc.) — Juvenile literature. 2. Recycling (Waste, etc.) — Juvenile literature. I. Title.
TD794.5 B37 2014
363.72—dc23

First Edition

Published in 2014 by
Gareth Stevens Publishing
111 East 14th Street, Suite 349
New York, NY 10003

© 2014 Gareth Stevens Publishing

Produced by Calcium, www.calciumcreative.co.uk
Designed by Simon Borrough and Paul Myerscough
Edited by Sarah Eason and Ruth Bennett

Photo credits: Cover: Shutterstock: Sunsetman. Inside: Dreamstime: Alangignoux 22, Americanspirit 21, Aneb 23, Cphoto 29, Daiphoto 11, Darknightsky 1, 12, Emersont 26, Harperdrewart 24, Hroephoto 17, Kev303 27b, Loraks 27t, Mangostock 28, Monamakela 20, Mosman11 13, Photka 19, Photobac 15, Stanko07 25, Stuarthe 18, Tashka 14; Shutterstock: Sergey Karpov 9, Hayati Kayhan 2, 16, khuruzero 10, Ulrich Mueller 4, Portokalis 7, Giuseppe R 5, Huguette Roe 6.

Printed in the United States of America

CPSIA compliance information: Batch #CS13GS: For further information contact Gareth Stevens,
New York, New York at 1-800-542-2595.

Contents

Waste   4

Where Does It All Go?   6

Why Recycle?   8

Recycling at Home   10

Glass   12

Plastics   14

Metals   16

Paper   18

Food and Garden Waste   20

Water   22

Household Waste   24

Energy from Waste   26

What Next?   28

Glossary   30

For More Information   31

Index   32

Waste

Every day of our lives we create waste, or something for which we no longer have a use. Although we think about what to do with our waste more now than ever before, we also produce more garbage than ever. But the good news is that our waste can be put to good use.

Throwaway Society

Many people living in wealthy countries have all sorts of possessions. Some are small, like cell phones, while others are large, like automobiles. Manufacturing all these things requires vast amounts of energy.

Most of our energy comes from fossil fuels—oil, coal, and natural gas. When these nonrenewable resources are burned, they release harmful substances, including greenhouse gases (GHGs). The greenhouse effect is causing world temperatures to rise, which is known as global warming. As well as these negative effects on the

What a waste. A lot of this "garbage" could have been repaired.

environment, fossil fuels also have to be mined, carefully refined, and made into various products, then transported to where they are needed. All of this requires yet more precious energy.

Rethinking Waste

In many cases, the products we buy are presented in all sorts of attractive containers and packaging. We throw away the packaging immediately, and when we've had enough of the product, we throw that away, too. As well as being garbage, waste is also throwing away things without thought. It is time to rethink waste and change our wasteful habits.

Developing Nations

People in poorer nations may not have an automobile, the latest cell phone, or a computer. Their lives are not as wasteful as those of people who live in wealthier regions. What is seen by many as waste is an opportunity in other places. Waste can be fixed, crafted into objects to sell, or used as materials to make into homes. These are some imaginative ways to recycle. Waste is used as something of value and recycling is a way of life.

Do you really need the latest cell phone? Or does your old one still work well enough?

Where Does It All Go?

Do you ever stop to think where waste goes? Our household garbage is taken away, almost like magic, every week. But unfortunately, our waste does not magically disappear. The garbage trucks take waste to a landfill site, a dump, or an incinerator. Recycling at home prevents us from discarding things as waste that can be used again.

Bury It

Landfill sites are large holes in the ground where waste is buried. They are filling up too quickly, and this can become hazardous. Although the waste is buried, rain still soaks through the soil, and poisonous chemicals drain into nearby land, rivers, and lakes. Modern landfill sites try to solve this by containing the poison, then removing it.

Huge landfill sites do not really solve the enormous problem of waste.

ECO FACT

Pile It High

When we dump our garbage it pollutes the countryside and can be harmful to wildlife. Imagine a huge pile of garbage that grows and grows—that's what a dump is. And an open dump is even more hazardous than a landfill site. Dumps swarm with flies and other vermin such as rats, which spread disease. However, waste mountains like this can be found all over the world.

Incineration

A lot of the world's waste gets burned in huge incinerators. Although burning waste makes heat energy, which can generate electricity, there are many problems. Plastics can release poisonous chemicals. Other substances create thick black smoke. Fumes from incineration contain harmful gases that need to be removed by filters, called scrubbers, before they are released into the atmosphere.

We notice waste a lot more if it is not collected regularly.

Why Recycle?

Recycling is all about using something again or making it into something new. Waste can be a useful resource for making other things. Today it's possible to recycle at least three-quarters of all our household waste. Most countries are nowhere near this figure—so we are missing the chance to make the world a cleaner and safer place for everyone.

The 3Rs

Recycling is one of the 3Rs. When it comes to waste, it is important to remember the 3Rs. They stand for:

- Reduce
- Reuse
- Recycle

Reduce waste by buying only things you really need. Try to buy fruit and vegetables without the unnecessary plastic packaging. Buy drinks in glass bottles, as it is easier to reuse or recycle glass than plastic.

Look for products with the recycling symbol and cut down on packaging.

8

Give Away, Use Again

Reuse items instead of throwing them away. Get your computer fixed rather than buying the latest model. If your bike is too small for you, give it away. Make a vase by decorating a large jar with glass paints.

Recycle anything for which you can no longer find a use. Plastic bottles can be shredded and turned into fleece jackets. There are people who make all sorts of original, fun recycled products from our waste.

There are all sorts of smart things you can do with used materials.

ECO FACT

3R Magic

Using the 3Rs of reduce, reuse, and recycle will help use up fewer natural resources, waste less, and create much less garbage. All of these valuable recyclable materials—including glass, paper, and metals—will then be taken to special recycling plants to be given another life. They will be made into something new and used again.

Recycling at Home

Waste is a global problem but recycling begins at home. We all have a responsibility to reduce the amount of resources we use, to reuse things, and to recycle. Every individual can make a worthwhile contribution by sorting waste at home and recycling.

This symbol tells you that a product or its packaging is recyclable.

Recycling Symbol

There are many types of waste products that can be recycled. Look out for the recycling symbol (of arrows arranged in a triangle) as a guide. Some of the most common recyclable items are glass bottles and jars, plastics, aluminum and steel cans, as well as paper and cardboard.

No Symbol?

No symbol? No problem. Many items, including electrical goods, such as cell phones, do not have a recycling symbol. But they can still be recycled! Many people upgrade their cell phones at least once a year. Handsets that still work can be passed on, and you can even make money from recycling a phone.

Give your old cell phone to a charity. It can be passed on to someone who can use it.

Sorting Up Close

We can all make our own small contribution. Wash cans, bottles, and containers for the recycling process. Crush aluminum drink cans so they take up less space in recycling bins. Always remove labels from cans and the tops from all bottles. Plastic tops from plastic bottles can also be recycled. Glass bottles and jars need to be sorted into their different types. Sorting at source—in other words, sorting at home before the items reach a recycling plant—helps to make the recycling process work efficiently.

Glass

Glass is an easy substance to recycle. It is made of sand and limestone, which are both readily available in the natural world. But these raw materials must be mined from the ground. If we recycle more glass, then we do not use so many natural resources. Glass can also be recycled over and over again.

Glass needs to be sorted into three main types—green, brown, and clear.

Making Glass

Sand and limestone are heated together in a furnace to temperatures of more than 21,600°F (12,000°C). The raw materials melt to form an extremely hot fluid mixture. This liquid is shaped into molds or blown into a shape. Then, it cools to make glass.

Glass Treatment Plants Up Close

Before we take glass bottles or jars to a recycling bin, we need to wash them and remove any tops or lids. There are only a few steps before new glass can be made.

- We sort glass bottles into their different colors at a recycling bin.
- Trucks take the sorted glass to a glass treatment plant.
- The glass is washed and crushed to form cullet.
- The cullet is heated in a furnace until it melts.
- Melted glass is molded into glass products, such as new bottles and jars.
- Other products can be made too, such as glass bricks, tiles, and fiberglass (used, for example, to make boats).

The fiberglass in this boat is a product made from glass.

Saving Energy

Recycling glass can be as simple as cleaning bottles and jars and filling them up again with the same or new products. Alternatively, glass bottles and jars can be recycled by smashing them to form cullet, and then melting them at a glass treatment plant. Melting cullet does not require such hot temperatures as the process of forming glass from sand and limestone. Recycling glass saves more than a quarter of the energy.

13

Plastics

Plastic is an extremely versatile material, as it is strong and durable. Many useful and important things are made from plastic. But the manufacture of plastic uses almost 10 percent of the planet's petroleum supplies, and only certain types of plastic are recycled.

In the United States, 5 percent of plastic is recycled. But we can save 1.8 tons (1.6 mt) of oil for every ton of recycled PET plastic.

What Sort of Plastic?

Most plastic water or soft-drink bottles (as well as some food packaging) are made from a strong, lightweight plastic called polyethylene terephthalate. It is better known as PET. Manufacturers stamp a code on the base of the bottle—PET or a number "1" inside a triangular recycling arrow. PET is 100 percent recyclable and can be made into all sorts of new products, including fibers for carpets.

Recycling Plastics Up Close

At the recycling plant, plastics are carefully sorted by hand.

- Plastics are sorted by type (1, 2, 3, and so on) and by color.
- The different types and colors of plastics are washed and chopped up.
- The plastic pieces are dropped into a water tank to be sorted again (some sink, others float).
- The plastic is dried, melted, and filtered to remove any unwanted pieces.
- The melted plastic is squeezed into long, thin pieces.
- The plastic strands are chopped up or spun into a fine fiber.

Would you wear plastic bottles? This fleece is made from them!

High-density polyethylene (or HDPE for short) is another plastic—it is used for many shampoo bottles and household cleaning products. HDPE plastics are stamped with the number "2." There are currently seven different types of recyclable plastic, but not all types are always recycled. Some plastic containers, such as margarine tubs, are harder to recycle than other containers because they may contain a combination of plastics.

15

Metals

Metals come from underground in the form of rocks called ores. They need to be mined, then heated in a furnace before the metal is in a form that we can use. Recycling metals cuts down on waste, energy use, and pollution.

Recycling one aluminum can conserves enough energy to run a TV for 3 hours.

Iron and Steel

Iron comes from iron ore, which is melted together with limestone and coke (from coal) in a furnace. If carbon and other minerals are added to the mixture, iron can be strengthened to make steel. Steel is used to make tough structures, such as bridges and buildings, as well as trains and ships. Most cans containing food products are also made from steel. Both steel and iron can be recycled very easily by being heated in a furnace.

Aluminum

What metal is your drink can made of? It's probably aluminum. Although it is thin and extremely light, aluminum is also tough. Aluminum comes from an ore called bauxite. The rocky ore is heated, producing a compound called alumina. In a process called smelting, an electrical current passes through the hot liquid alumina to separate the aluminum metal.

North America has been recycling steel for more than 150 years.

Recycling Aluminum Up Close

Unlike iron or steel, aluminum is not magnetic. At recycling plants, giant magnets can be used to remove any unwanted steel cans.

- Cans are crushed at pressure to make huge aluminum bales.
- Aluminum bales are melted in a furnace at a temperature of about 1,300°F (704°C), which is three times hotter than a pizza oven.
- The molten metal is poured into molds to make large aluminum ingots.
- The ingots are rolled into thin sheets to make new products, such as drink cans and foil food containers.
- Recycling aluminum saves 95 percent of the energy needed to make fresh aluminum from raw materials.

Paper

To make paper you need trees, but also vast amounts of water. Recycling paper not only helps to conserve these natural resources, but it also protects animals in wild forests and saves space in landfills.

For every ton of paper you recycle, you save about 15 trees.

Making Paper

To make paper, trees are chopped down and processed into wood chips. These are then mixed with water to form a pulp. This process breaks down the wood chips into fibers. The pulp gets rolled out and flattened in order to squeeze out the water. It is then cut into sheets and dried, making paper.

Recycling Paper Up Close

Paper is transported to a paper recycling plant to be made into... paper!

- Paper and cardboard is sorted, depending on its type or quality.
- It is pulped using water, chemicals, and heat.
- The pulp is cleaned, then filtered and spun at high speed.
- Ink is removed by washing the pulp or by passing air through it.
- The pulp is bleached (if the final product is going to be white paper).
- It is sprayed with lots of water on a fast-moving flat surface.
- The wood fibers stick together as the water drains away.
- The mushy pulp is squashed flat into sheets, squeezing out any excess water.
- The paper sheets are ironed, rolled, and allowed to dry, to make recycled paper.

Recycled paper can be used to make goods such as store bags.

Recycling Paper

A similar process happens when recycling paper. This time, used paper replaces the wood chips. Paper is first sorted into different types, such as magazines, newspapers, office paper, and cardboard. The paper is mixed with water to make pulp. It takes less water to make pulp from recycled paper than from wood chips.

Food and Garden Waste

Garden waste and most kinds of food garbage, such as fruit and vegetable peelings, are biodegradable. In other words, unlike plastics and glass, they can decay or rot. All they need are the right conditions, and a little bit of time.

Compost

A rich, dirt-like substance called compost is nature's way of recycling. Invertebrates and tiny microorganisms break down plants and organic waste in the soil. The nutrients return to the soil, making it richer. As well as microorganisms and nutrients, compost needs air, water, and enough time to allow it to rot.

Vegetable peelings and scraps are perfect materials for compost.

Composting Up Close

It is quite easy to make compost at home. Create an open heap in the garden, set up a small bin, or make a compost enclosure from wood or old tires.

- Cover the base with small branches, providing gaps to allow air in and water out.
- Add food scraps and garden waste in layers, if you can. Microorganisms in the compost heap break down the organic waste, making heat in the process.
- Cover your compost heap with a piece of old carpet or sheet of plastic to keep in the heat, and protect it from rainwater.
- Gradually, the compost at the bottom of the heap will be ready—look out for black, crumbly dirt.

Community Composting

In the same way, food waste can be recycled effectively. Many neighborhoods operate roadside schemes to collect food and garden waste from our homes. The waste is transported to a special facility to make compost. This organic waste can be sold or given away.

If you have no space in your backyard for compost, find your local neighborhood site.

Water

Do you know about the water cycle? Rain falls, water runs off into rivers and down to the oceans, then evaporates to form clouds, before falling as rain again. In this way, water gets naturally recycled every day. But did you realize that wastewater can also be recycled?

Saving Water

Most living creatures will die without water. But in water-rich countries where water is readily available, many people take water for granted, as it appears whenever they turn on a tap. In other countries, where the climate is hot and dry, water is not so easy to find. We should all be careful to conserve water, however, as this amazing liquid is the most precious resource in the world.

Many people do not have access to clean water from a running tap.

Wastewater

It may seem strange, but even wastewater is precious. Filthy water from your sinks, baths, and toilets goes to a sewage plant, where it is cleaned. The water can then flow back into rivers and oceans. Water is always cleaned at a water treatment plant before it reaches your home as fresh water.

In sewage treatment plants, filter beds allow heavy sediment to fall to the bottom.

Sewage Treatment Up Close

A sewage treatment plant ensures that wastewater is properly cleaned before it goes back into the environment.

- Wastewater from our homes empties into drains, which run into the sewage treatment plant.
- A grid or filter removes solid waste.
- Filter beds lined with sand and gravel separate large particles from the water.
- Bacteria (tiny living things) feed on the harmful microbes, cleaning the water.
- Water settles in tanks and is filtered again.
- Water, disinfected with UV light or chlorine, is tested by scientists to make sure there are no remaining germs.
- Clean water is returned to rivers, lakes, and oceans.

Household Waste

We even throw away big and expensive items—if we want to get a better version, for example. Electrical items, such as TVs and computers, take up a lot of space in landfill sites. Discarded electrical equipment can also be very dangerous. It can produce poisonous chemicals if it is incinerated or sent to a landfill. We can avoid this by recycling.

Computers can be recycled. Even broken equipment can be taken apart and used.

E-Waste

Electrical waste, or e-waste, is a major problem around the world. "White goods," such as fridges, washing machines, and stoves, make up the majority of e-waste, followed by computer equipment and TVs. E-waste makes up 5 percent of all the solid waste produced across the world.

ECO FACT

Good as New

Many discarded electrical items still work, or can be fixed. Reusing electronic equipment should be the first option, as it saves energy and does not waste new materials. If they cannot be fixed, then parts (keyboards or disk drives, for example) could be reused.

You can find all sorts of great "one-off" clothes at thrift stores.

Clothes and Textiles

Textiles (woven or knitted cloth, including clothing) is another large part of household waste. Used clothes and fabrics can be recycled by taking them to a thrift store.

If clothes cannot be sold, they can still be recycled. They can be shredded and then spun into new fiber for weaving and knitting. Poor-quality fibers can be used for carpet underlay or cushion stuffing.

25

Energy from Waste

All sorts of waste products can be recycled—even animal manure. Manure can be used as a soil fertilizer for crops or burned to make electricity. Biogas can also be collected from animal manure as it decomposes or rots.

Biogas

Animal manure gives off biogas as it starts to rot. This natural process of decay can be a source of fuel. Methane, part of biogas, is a greenhouse gas that is contributing to global warming, so collecting the gas (rather than letting it escape into the atmosphere) is good for the environment. A special tank called a biogas digester is used to collect biogas for fuel. Fresh manure is added to the biogas digester, where it is covered and starved of oxygen. Natural bacteria help to ferment the manure, and as the waste rots, methane is released. The gas can then be piped away and used as a fuel for cooking and heating.

Collecting harmful methane produced by cattle is recycling in action.

Biogas plants are on the rise as an alternative energy source.

How Rotten!

In the same way that dead plants break down over time in a compost heap, organic matter in landfill sites also starts to decompose. This rotting process produces gases, including methane, which can be collected. By reusing this waste product, we are saving our natural resources and not harming the environment by mining coal or natural gas.

ECO FACT

Poop Power!

Animal manure, such as chicken droppings, can be used in power stations. The manure is incinerated, or burned, with temperatures rising to about 1,560°F (849°C). The high temperatures heat water in a boiler, producing steam. The steam turns a turbine, which is connected to an electrical generator. This produces electricity, which can then be used by thousands of local homes.

What Next?

Recycling does have costs—for transporting waste and operating recycling plants. But recycling saves money, and conserves energy and natural resources. Together we need to make recycling a way of life, all over the world. If we don't, it may eventually cost us the Earth.

It is often volunteers that tidy our beaches. Sixty percent of the garbage is plastic.

Recycling Works

Recycling is a way to start putting something back into our planet, instead of creating more and more waste. We all have a responsibility to recycle our own waste. But recycling also needs to keep moving forward—we need to think of new and better ways to do it.

New Products from Old

A new fleece jacket can be made from 25 recycled plastic bottles. That's ingenious, isn't it? But we will not be able to save the world by buying fleece jackets! Consumers will buy recyclable products, but only if they are useful, attractive, and priced well. Designers and creative thinkers will need to continue to find all sorts of exciting new products that can be made from our old recycled products. Who said it was just a load of old garbage?

Cut down on your own waste—and encourage friends to do the same.

ECO FACT

Zero Waste

Zero Waste is an initiative to design products that are specially manufactured to be repaired, reused, or recycled. The aim of Zero Waste is ultimately to reduce waste to nothing. While this may never be achieved, it is a worthy goal and we can all help. Make every day a recycling day, and persuade others to see how important it is to reduce, reuse, and recycle waste.

Glossary

bales large bundles or packages bound together

bauxite ore containing the metal aluminum

biodegradable able to rot away naturally

biogas a gas produced when living things rot

biogas digester a device used to collect methane from rotting animal waste

chlorine a strong chemical often used as a disinfectant

community a group of people living in one area, for example, a neighborhood

conserve to save

cullet a crushed form of glass (used to make glass again)

decompose to break down or rot

discard to throw away, get rid of

disinfected cleaned, destroying diseases and germs

energy usable power, such as electricity

environment surroundings

evaporates turns into vapor or gas

fertilizer a substance used to make soil richer

furnace a very hot oven

global warming the rise in Earth's temperatures, caused by greenhouse gases

greenhouse gases gases in the air that trap heat like a greenhouse

hazardous dangerous

incinerate to burn

ingots blocks of metal

initiative the first step taken to start something

invertebrates bugs or creatures without backbones

methane a colorless, odorless greenhouse gas

microorganisms tiny living creatures

nutrients substances needed by plants or animals, which can return to the soil when they die

ore rock containing a metal

organic to do with living organisms

petroleum crude oil, a thick liquid from under the ground

pollutes makes air, water, or land dirty

pulp a mixture of wood fibers and water

recycling plant a building used for recycling materials

resources raw materials used to make something

sewage waste matter in sewers

smelting melting ore to obtain the metal

textiles any cloth made by knitting or weaving

turbine a machine that is turned by water, steam, or air

UV light ultra-violet light, used in a process to clean water

vermin animals or bugs seen as troublesome to humans, such as rats and cockroaches

For More Information

Books

Hewitt, Sally. *Waste and Recycling*. New York, NY: Crabtree, 2008.

Lucas Donald, Rhonda. *Recycling*. New York, NY: Children's Press, 2002.

Stark, Edwin. *The Recycling Kid*. Killer Squirrel Press, Kindle edition, 2011.

Threadgould, Tiffany. *ReMake It! Recycling Projects from the Stuff You Usually Scrap*. New York, NY: Sterling, 2011.

Websites

Check out the games, ideas, and stories at:
kids.nationalgeographic.co.uk/kids/games/actiongames/recycle-roundup

Take a look at this fun website that explains how we can look after the planet:
www.meetthegreens.org

There is a drag-and-drop game and much more on the My Garbology website:
www.naturebridge.org/garbology.php

Index

3Rs 8, 9

alumina 17
aluminum 10, 11, 16, 17

bacteria 23, 26
bauxite 17
biodegradable 20
biogas 26
biogas digester 26

cardboard 10, 19
cell phones 4, 5, 11
chicken droppings 27
clothes 25
coke (coal) 16
compost 20, 21
compost heap 21, 27
computers 5, 9, 24
cullet 13

decay 20, 26
dumps 6, 7

electrical goods 11, 24, 25
energy 4, 5, 7, 13, 16, 17, 25, 26–27, 28
e-waste 24

fertilizer 26
fleece jackets 9, 15, 29
foil 17
food waste 20–21
furnace 12, 13, 16, 17

garden waste 20–21
glass 8, 9, 10, 11, 12–13, 20
glass treatment plant 13
global warming 4, 26
greenhouse gas 4, 26

HDPE 15
household waste 6, 8, 10, 21, 24–25

incineration 6, 7, 24, 27
iron 16, 17

landfill sites 6, 7, 18, 24, 27
limestone 12, 13, 16

manure 26, 27
metals 9, 16–17
methane 26, 27
microorganisms 20, 21, 23

nutrients 20

ores 16, 17
organic waste 20, 21, 27

paper 9, 10, 18–19
PET 14
petroleum 14
plastics 7, 8, 9, 10, 11, 14–15, 20, 21, 28, 29
pollution 7, 16
pulp 18, 19

recycling bins 11, 13
recycling plant 9, 11, 15, 17, 19, 28
recycling symbol 8, 10, 11, 14
reduce 8, 9, 10, 29
reuse 8, 9, 10, 25, 29
rotting 20, 26, 27

sand 12, 13, 23
sewage 23
sewage treatment plant 23
smelting 17
sorting at source 10, 11
steel 10, 16, 17

textiles 25
trees 18

waste 4–5, 6, 7, 8, 9, 10, 16, 20, 21, 22, 23, 24, 25, 26, 27, 28, 29
wastewater 22, 23
water cycle 22
wood 18, 19, 21

zero waste 29